David & Charles
Cross Stitch Collection

A DAVID & CHARLES BOOK

First published in the UK in 2004

Designs copyright © Christine Lovell, Jayne Netley Mayhew, Helen Philipps 2004
Text, layout, photographs copyright © David & Charles 2004

Distributed in North America by F&W Publications, Inc. 4700 East Galbraith Road Cincinnati, OH 45236 1-800-289-0963

Christine Lovell, Jayne Netley Mayhew and Helen Philipps have asserted their right to be identified as authors of this work in accordance with the Copyright, Designs and Patents Act, 1988.

The publisher has endeavoured to contact all contributors of text and pictures for permission to reproduce.

ISBN 0 7153 1753 9

A catalogue record for this book is available from the British Library.

Printed in Singapore by KHL Printing Co Pte Ltd
for D_____ & Ch_____
                wton Abbot Devon

            at
arles.co.uk

books are
good book

er flowers

Summer Flowers

Contents

The Stitched Designs	2–3
SUMMER GARDEN SAMPLER	4–5
FLOWER GARLAND	6–7
ROSE GARDEN, ROSE AND ROSEBUD	8–9
SUNFLOWERS	10
FOXGLOVES	11–13
Stitching Advice	14–16

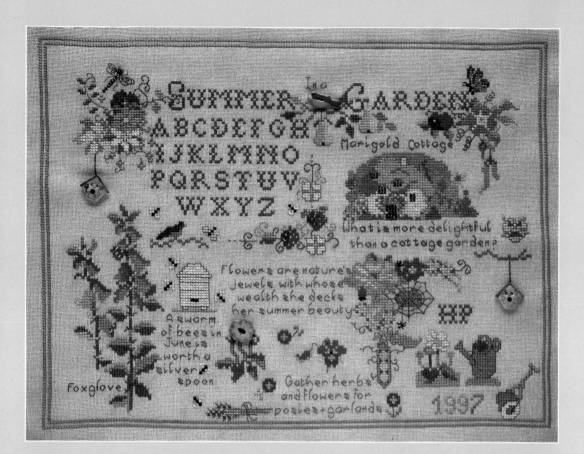

Summer Garden
Sampler
© Helen Philipps

Flower Garland
© Jayne Netley Mayhew

Rose Garden
© Christine Lovell

Sunflowers
© Jayne Netley Mayhew

Rose and Rosebud
© Christine Lovell

Foxgloves
© Jayne Netley Mayhew

Summer

A B C D E F G H
I J K L M N O
P Q R S T U V
W X Y Z

In a

Flowers are nature'
jewels with whose
wealth she decks
her summer beaut

A swarm
of bees in
June is
worth a
silver
spoon

Gather he
and flowers
posies + gar

Foxglove

4

Summer Garden Sampler

DMC STRANDED COTTON

CROSS STITCH		BACKSTITCH	
□	92	⁄	114
\	114	⁄	310
H	211	⁄	317
▬	310	⁄	318
→	317	⁄	469
∩	318	⁄	471
𝅘	433	⁄	501
+	469	□	712
U	471	⁄	718
ᔑ	501	⁄	794
▽	503	⁄	816
·	712	⁄	972
◄	718	⁄	3607
T	726	⁄	3746
S	794	⁄	3826
⊥	796		
▨	814	**FRENCH KNOTS**	
✕	816	●	114
▬	957	□	712
○	963	▨	726
K	970		
◎	972	**BEADS**	
L	3607	●	310
✕	3608	●	blue
÷	3716	▢	crystal
↑	3746		
‖	3808		
Z	3826		
ⅎ	3827		

Add your initials and date using the alphabet within the sampler and the numbers charted, in the colour of your choice

---

SUMMER GARDEN SAMPLER	
STITCH COUNT	193 x 148
DESIGN SIZE	35 x 27cm (13¾ x 10½in)
FABRIC USED	Evenweave 28-count cream, over 2 fabric threads
THREADS USED	See key: 2 strands stranded cotton (floss) for cross stitch, 1 strand for French knots & backstitch, 1 strand for backstitch lettering
EMBELLISHMENTS (OPTIONAL)	Buttons: 2 birdhouses, 1 pansy, 1 bluebird (or stitch motifs instead) Seed beads: pale blue, black, crystal

FLOWER GARLAND

STITCH COUNTS	129 x 130 (garland), 48 x 48 (triple fuchsia) and 26 x 34 (single fuchsia)
DESIGN SIZES	Garland: 33 x 33cm (13 x 13in) on 20-count 23.5 x 23.5cm (9¼ x 9¼in) on 28-count Triple fuchsia: 12.2 x 12.2cm (4¾ x 4¾in) on 24-count Single fuchsia: 6.6 x 8.6cm (2½ x 3½in) on 24-count
FABRIC USED	Evenweave 20-count (or 28-count) antique white or sage green, over 2 fabric threads
THREADS USED	See key: 3 strands stranded cotton (floss) for cross stitch & 2 strands for backstitch on 20-count (2 strands and 1 strand on 24-count)

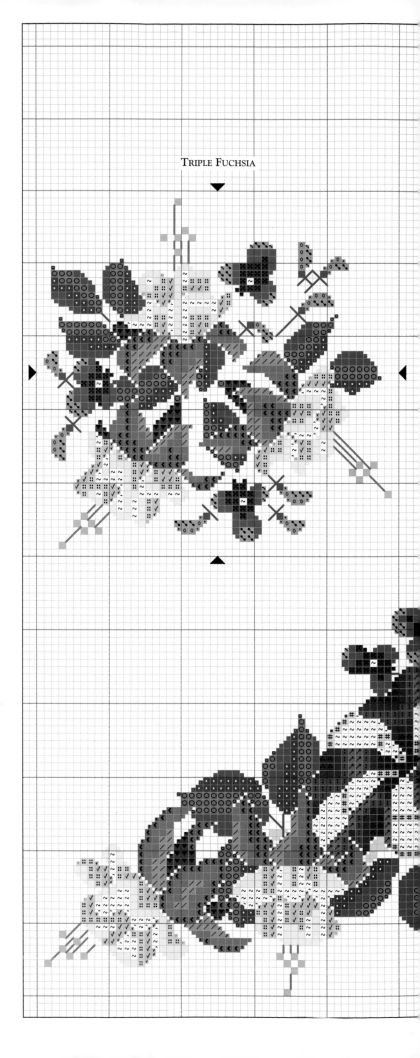

TRIPLE FUCHSIA

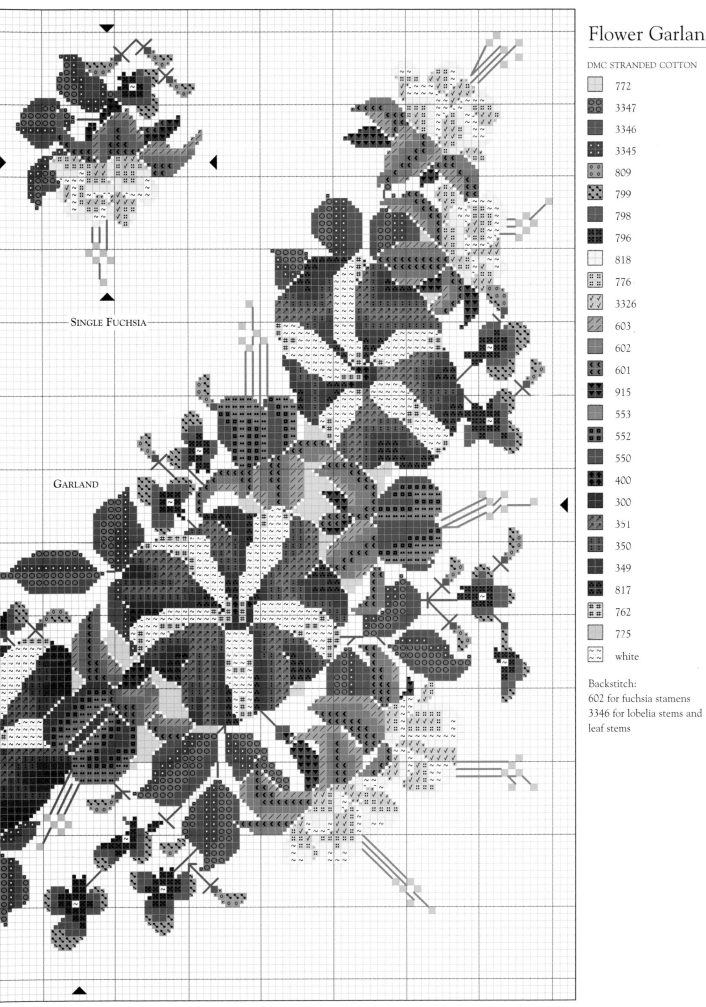

Flower Garland

DMC STRANDED COTTON

	772
	3347
	3346
	3345
	809
	799
	798
	796
	818
	776
	3326
	603
	602
	601
	915
	553
	552
	550
	400
	300
	351
	350
	349
	817
	762
	725
	white

Backstitch:
602 for fuchsia stamens
3346 for lobelia stems and
leaf stems

SINGLE FUCHSIA

GARLAND

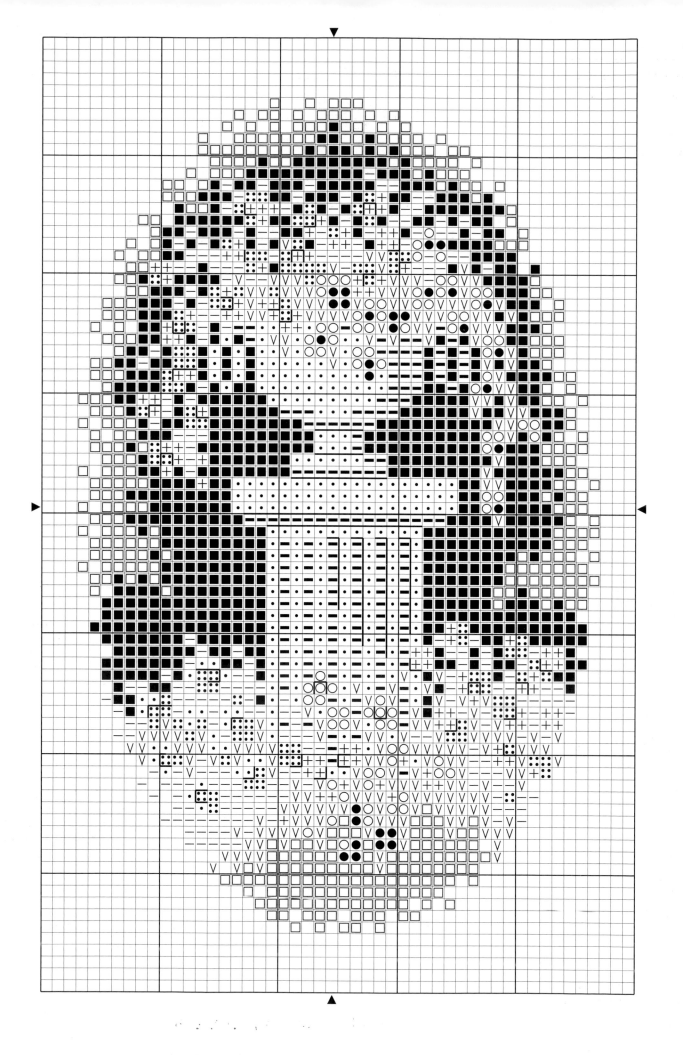

Rose (right)

ANCHOR STRANDED COTTON

·	Lemon yellow	292
△	Orange yellow	313
+	Orange pink	328
−	Deep pink	11
●	Plum	59
		Pale green	241
::	Light green	243
□	Medium green	244
■	Dark green	246

Backstitch outline: one strand of plum 59

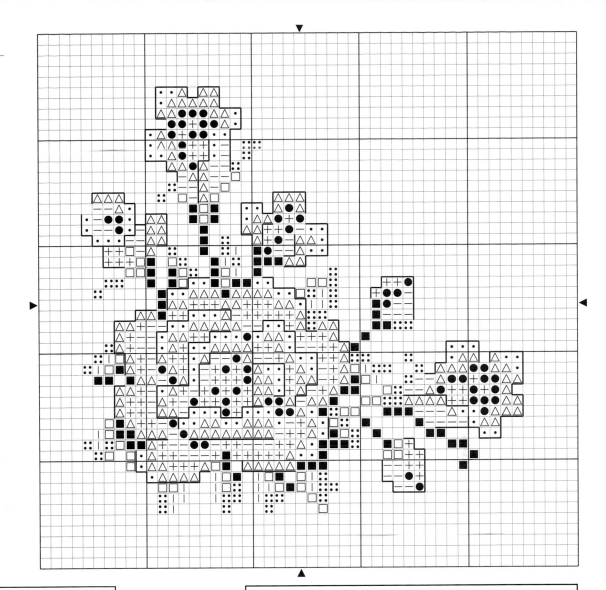

<table>
<tr><td colspan="3">ROSE GARDEN</td></tr>
<tr><td>STITCH COUNT</td><td colspan="2">44 x 70</td></tr>
<tr><td>DESIGN SIZE</td><td colspan="2">8 x 12.7cm (3⅛ x 5in)</td></tr>
<tr><td>FABRIC USED</td><td colspan="2">Aida 14-count mint, over 1 block</td></tr>
<tr><td>THREADS USED</td><td colspan="2">See key: 3 strands stranded cotton (floss) for cross stitch, 2 strands for backstitch on urn & pedestal, 1 strand backstitch on flowers</td></tr>
</table>

<table>
<tr><td colspan="2">ROSE AND ROSEBUD</td></tr>
<tr><td>STITCH COUNTS</td><td>41 x 40 & 12 x 15</td></tr>
<tr><td>DESIGN SIZES</td><td>7.4 x 7.4cm (3 x 3in) & 2 x 2.7cm (⅞ x 1in)</td></tr>
<tr><td>FABRIC USED</td><td>Aida 14-count mint, over 1 block</td></tr>
<tr><td>THREADS USED</td><td>See key: 2 strands of stranded cotton (floss) for cross stitch, 1 strand for backstitch</td></tr>
</table>

Rose Garden (left)

ANCHOR STRANDED COTTON

·	Lemon yellow	292
−	Mustard	874
::	Orange yellow	313
+	Orange pink	328
−	Deep pink	11
●	Plum	59
		Pale green	241
V	Light green	243
□	Medium green	244
■	Dark green	246

Backstitch outline: one strand of dark green 246 on urn and pedestal; one strand of plum 59 for flowers

Rosebud (right)

ANCHOR STRANDED COTTON

·	Lemon yellow	292
△	Orange yellow	313
+	Orange pink	328
−	Deep pink	11
●	Plum	59
::	Light green	243
□	Medium green	244
■	Dark green	246

Backstitch outline: one strand of plum 59

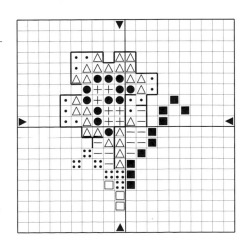

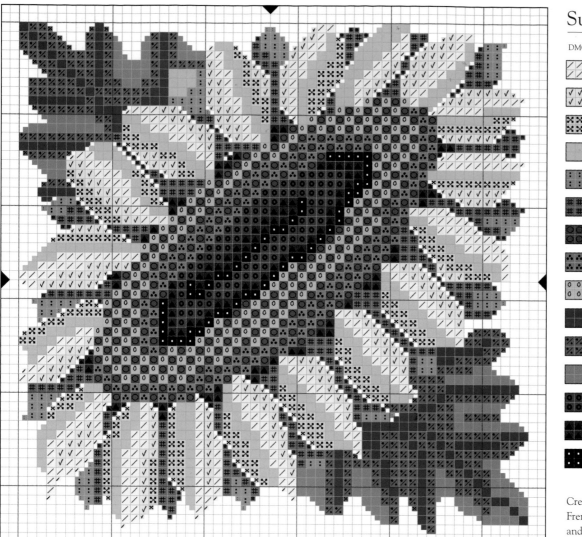

Sunflowers

DMC STRANDED COTTON

3078	
727	
726	
725	
783	
781	
975	
976	
742	
936	
580	
581	
433	
898	
310	

Create texture by working French knots in 975, 976 and 742 instead of the cross stitches of the same colour

SILK RIBBON PETALS

— 7mm light yellow
— 7mm dark yellow

SUNFLOWERS	
STITCH COUNTS	55 x 55 and 40 x 40
DESIGN SIZES	10 x 10cm (4 x 4in) and 7.3 x 7.3cm (2⅞ x 2⅞in)
FABRIC USED	Aida 14-count white or yellow, over 1 block
THREADS USED	See key: 2 strands stranded cotton (floss) for cross stitch and French knots. On the smaller sunflower work the petals in alternating silk ribbon straight stitches
EMBELLISHMENTS	7mm silk ribbons

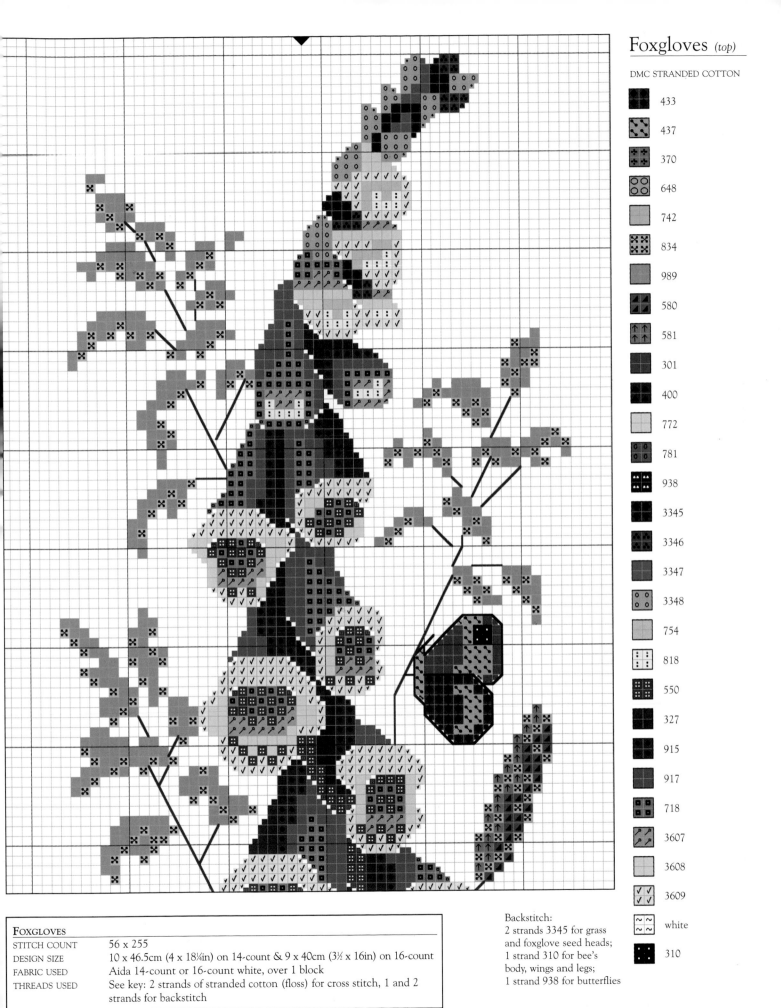

Foxgloves (top)

DMC STRANDED COTTON

Symbol	Code
	433
	437
	370
	648
	742
	834
	989
	580
	581
	301
	400
	772
	781
	938
	3345
	3346
	3347
	3348
	754
	818
	550
	327
	915
	917
	718
	3607
	3608
	3609
	white
	310

Backstitch:
2 strands 3345 for grass
and foxglove seed heads;
1 strand 310 for bee's
body, wings and legs;
1 strand 938 for butterflies

FOXGLOVES

STITCH COUNT	56 x 255
DESIGN SIZE	10 x 46.5cm (4 x 18¼in) on 14-count & 9 x 40cm (3½ x 16in) on 16-count
FABRIC USED	Aida 14-count or 16-count white, over 1 block
THREADS USED	See key: 2 strands of stranded cotton (floss) for cross stitch, 1 and 2 strands for backstitch

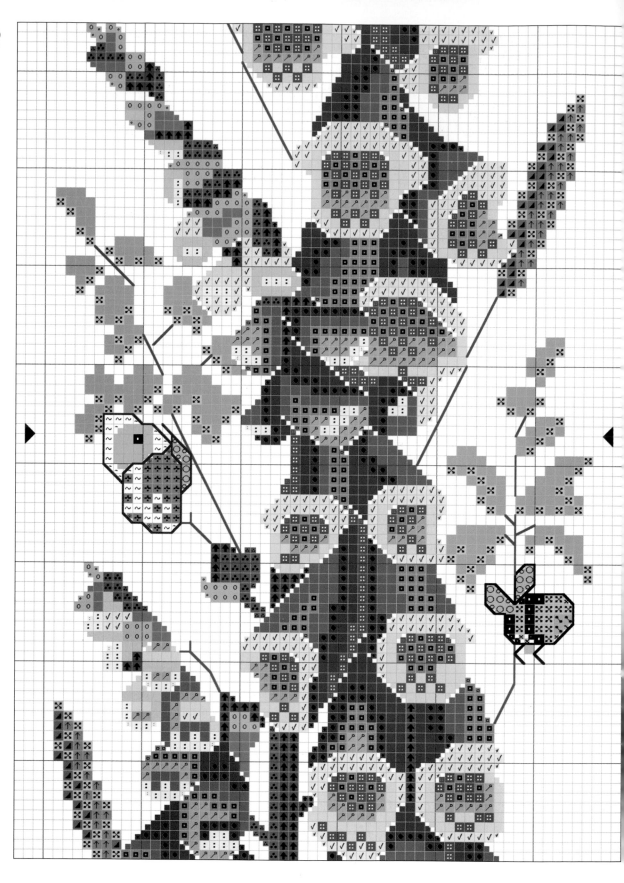

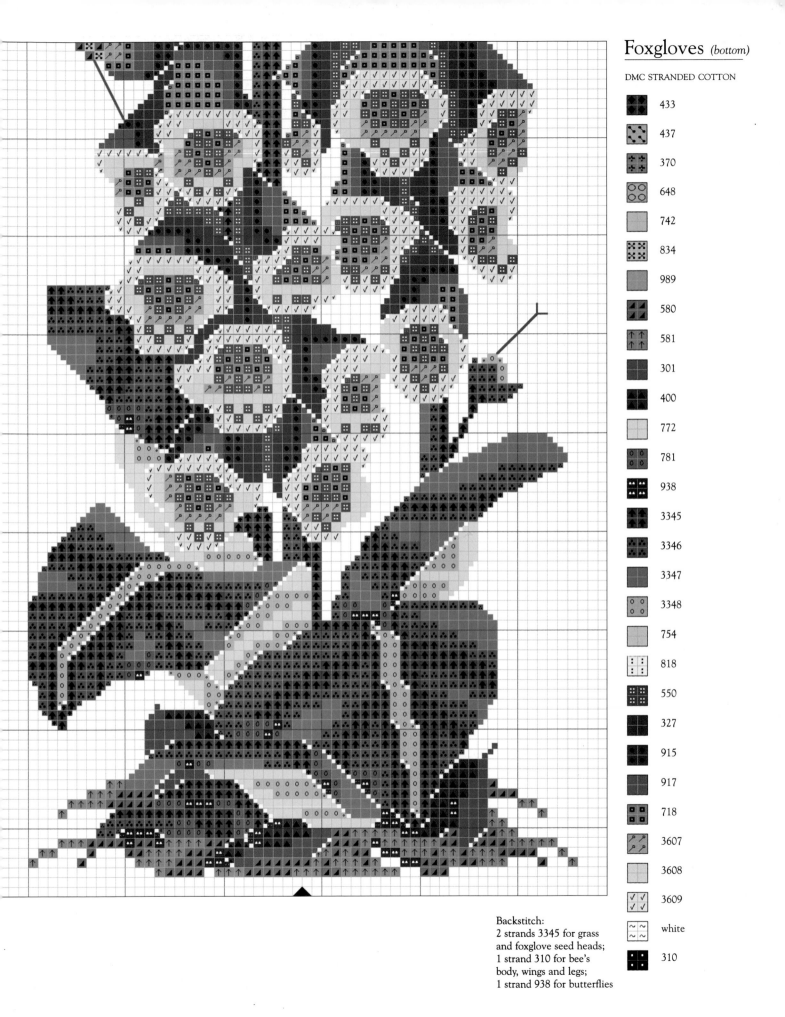

DMC STRANDED COTTON

■	433
▨	437
▦	370
○○	648
	742
▨	834
	989
◪	580
↑↑	581
	301
	400
	772
○○	781
▦	938
▦	3345
▦	3346
	3347
○○	3348
	754
:.:	818
▦	550
	327
	915
	917
▪▪	718
◢	3607
	3608
√√	3609
~~	white
▦	310

Backstitch:
2 strands 3345 for grass
and foxglove seed heads;
1 strand 310 for bee's
body, wings and legs;
1 strand 938 for butterflies

Stitching Advice

The following section is relevant throughout the David & Charles *Cross Stitch Collection* series, not just the charts in this book. It will provide you with all the information you need to stitch the designs charted.

MATERIALS

FABRICS

Fabrics used for counted cross stitch are woven so they have the same number of threads or blocks to 2.5cm (1in), both horizontally and vertically. The two main fabric types used are blockweaves such as Aida, and evenweaves such as linen. Cross stitch can also be worked on other fabrics such as waste canvas, plastic canvas and stitching (perforated) paper.

AIDAS These fabrics are woven in blocks and are available in many colours and counts – 8, 11, 14, 16, 18 and 20 blocks to 2.5cm (1in). They are made from various fibres and as different width bands. When stitching on Aida, one block on the fabric corresponds to one square on a chart and each cross stitch is worked over one block.

EVENWEAVES These fabrics are woven singly and are made from various fibres and as different width bands. They are also available in many different colours and counts. When stitching on evenweave, each cross stitch is usually worked over two threads of the fabric.

WASTE CANVAS This is designed for stitching on fabrics where cross stitching wouldn't normally be possible because the threads are uneven, such as clothing. To use, tack (baste) a piece of waste canvas large enough for the design into position on to the chosen article and cross stitch the design through both fabrics. When all stitching is complete, dampen the canvas and use tweezers to draw out the threads. You may find it easier to work backstitches after the canvas has been removed.

PLASTIC CANVAS This is a rigid but flexible mesh-like material that can be cut and assembled into three-dimensional objects. It is available in various counts and as pre-cut shapes. Cross stitches are worked over intersections of the mesh.

STITCHING PAPER Cross stitch designs can be worked on perforated paper which can then be cut, folded and glued to make a variety of items such as cards, bookmarks and notebook covers. The right side is the smoother side of the paper and cross stitch is normally worked with three strands of stranded cotton (floss) and backstitch with two.

THREADS

The most commonly used thread for counted embroidery is stranded cotton (floss) but there are many other types available, including rayons, space-dyed or variegated threads, perlé cottons and metallic threads.

STRANDED COTTON (FLOSS) This six-stranded thread can be bought by the skein in hundreds of colours with ranges made by DMC, Anchor and Madeira (see DMC/Anchor conversion chart at the front of this book). Colours can be mixed or 'tweeded' in the needle. The stitching information with the charts will tell you how many strands to use for a design.

VARIEGATED THREADS There are many lovely variegated threads available now. The chart keys give the name and code of the thread used. When stitching with variegated threads work cross stitches as complete stitches, not in two journeys or the colour sequence will be spoiled.

METALLICS AND BLENDING FILAMENTS Metallic threads are available in many gorgeous colours and finishes from various companies and they can be used in cross stitch designs to create glitter and interest. Blending filaments can be stitched with stranded cotton (floss) to create an overall sparkle to a design. Use shorter lengths of thread when working with metallics to avoid tangles and excessive wear on the thread.

TAPESTRY WOOL (YARN) Many cross stitch designs can be stitched on canvas in tapestry wool (yarn) instead of stranded cotton (floss), using half cross stitch or tent stitch instead of cross stitch. Ask at needlework shops for suppliers and colour conversions from stranded cotton (floss).

EQUIPMENT

Very little equipment is needed for cross stitch embroidery and the following basics are all you need to get you started.

NEEDLES Use blunt tapestry needles for counted cross stitch. The commonest sizes used are 24 and 26 but the size depends on your project and personal preference. Avoid leaving a needle in the fabric unless it is gold plated or it may cause marks. A beading needle (or fine 'sharp' needle), which is much thinner, will be needed to attach beads.

SCISSORS Use dressmaker's shears for cutting fabric and a small, sharp pair of pointed scissors for cutting embroidery threads.

FRAMES AND HOOPS These are not essential but if you use one, choose one large enough to hold the complete design, to avoid marking the fabric and flattening stitches.

TECHNIQUES

USING CHARTS

The designs in this series are worked from black and white charts with symbols, or colour charts with a black and/or white symbol to aid colour identification. Each square, both occupied and unoccupied, represents one block of Aida or two threads of linen, unless stated otherwise. Each occupied square equals one cross stitch. Some charts also have three-quarter cross stitches (sometimes called fractional stitches) and these usually occupy part of a square, either a triangle or a small square. French knots are indicated by circles, usually coloured in the colour charts and labelled in the key or on the chart. Backstitch (and sometimes long stitch) is shown on charts by straight lines, usually coloured in the colour charts, with the code either on the chart or in the key. Arrows at the sides of the charts allow you to find the centre easily.

CALCULATING DESIGN SIZE

Each project gives the stitch count and finished design size but if you plan to work the design on a different count you will need to be able to calculate the finished size. To do this, count the number of stitches in the design and divide this by the fabric count number, e.g., 140 stitches x 140 stitches ÷ by 14-count = a design size of 10 x 10in (25.4 x 25.4cm). Remember that working on evenweave usually means working over two threads not one, so divide the fabric count by 2 before you start. See the bottom of page 15 for a quick stitch count table.

PREPARING FABRICS

The sizes given with the charts are for the finished design size only, therefore you will need to add about 10–12.5cm (4–5in) to both measurements when cutting embroidery fabric, to allow enough fabric around the edges for working and for making up later.

Before you begin stitching, press your embroidery fabric if necessary and trim the selvage or any rough edges. Work from the middle of the fabric and middle of the chart where possible to ensure your design is centred on the fabric. Find the middle of the fabric by folding it in four and pressing lightly. Mark the folds with tailor's chalk or with lines of tacking (basting) following a fabric thread. When working with linen, prepare as described above but also sew a narrow hem around all raw edges to preserve them for finishing later.

STARTING AND FINISHING STITCHING

Unless indicated otherwise, begin stitching in the middle of a design to ensure an adequate margin for making up. Start and finish stitching neatly, avoiding knots which create a lumps.

KNOTLESS LOOP START This start can be used with an even number of strands i.e., 2, 4 or 6. To stitch with two strands, begin with one strand about 80cm (30in). Double the thread and thread the needle with the two ends. Put the needle up through the fabric from the wrong side, where you intend to begin stitching, leaving the loop at the back (see diagram top of page 15). Form a half cross stitch, put the needle back through the fabric and through the waiting loop to anchor the stitch.

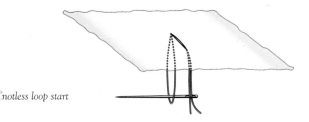

knotless loop start

AWAY WASTE KNOT START Start this way if using an odd number of strands. Thread the needle with the number of strands required and knot the end. Insert the needle into the right side of the fabric, away from where you wish to begin stitching (see diagram below). Stitch towards the knot and cut it off when the threads are anchored. Alternatively, snip off the knot, thread a needle and work under a few stitches to anchor.

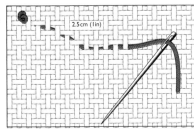

away waste knot start

FINISHING STITCHING At the back of the work, pass the needle and thread under several stitches and snip off the loose end close to the stitching. Begin new colours by passing through stitches on the back in a similar way.

NUMBER OF STRANDS

Stranded cotton (floss) is available in six-stranded skeins and different numbers of strands will be needed for use on different gauges of fabric. Generally two strands are used for cross stitch and one for backstitch but the following table gives further advice.

HOW MANY STRANDS?	
FABRIC	NUMBER OF STRANDS OF STRANDED COTTON
6-count Aida	6 or 8 for cross stitch, 2 for backstitch
8-count Aida	6 for cross stitch, 2 for backstitch
11-count Aida & 22-count evenweave (over 2 threads)	3 for cross stitch, 1 for backstitch
14-count Aida & 28-count evenweave (over 2 threads)	2 or 3 for cross stitch, 1 for backstitch
16-count Aida & 32-count evenweave (over 2 threads)	2 for cross stitch, 1 for backstitch
18-count Aida & 36-count evenweave (over 2 threads)	1 or 2 for cross stitch, 1 for backstitch

BLENDING THREADS

Many threads can be used together in the needle to create new colour combinations or to add the shine and glitter of metallic threads such as blending filament. Simply thread the needle with both threads, usually one strand of each, and stitch as normal.

CHANGING NAMES AND DATES

Some cross stitch designs feature names and dates or other wording which you will need to alter using the alphabet provided (or one of your own favourites). Before you begin to stitch, ensure the words will fit the space by counting the squares in the space available (width and height) and marking this on square graph paper. Pencil the letters or numbers on the graph paper, remembering the spaces between letters and words.

ATTACHING BEADS, CHARMS AND BUTTONS

Bead positions are shown on the charts as circles (coloured in the colour charts), with details of the bead type in the key. You might find using a frame or hoop is helpful to keep the fabric taut as you pull the thread firmly to keep the beads in position. Attach beads using a beading needle or very fine 'sharp' needle, thread which matches the bead colour and a half cross stitch (or a full cross stitch if you prefer).

Charm and button positions are usually shown on the chart or described in the key or shown on the photograph of the model. Attach charms and buttons with matching thread.

If you cannot find the beads, charms or buttons suggested on the charts simply substitute something else – there is a wealth to choose from nowadays.

USING RIBBON

Narrow ribbon can be used to create additional interest in a cross stitch design. It may be used to form stitches, such as simple straight stitches, lazy daisy stitch or detached chain stitch. It can also be couched flat on to the fabric and held in place with cross stitches or narrow straight stitches or beads. Ribbon can also be threaded through evenweave fabric after several threads have been removed to create a channel.

TIPS FOR PERFECT STITCHING

- Organize your threads before you start a project as this will help to avoid confusion later. Always include the manufacturer's name and the shade number.

- Separate the strands on a skein of stranded cotton (floss) before taking the number you need to stitch with. Realign them before threading your needle.

- If using a frame, try to avoid a hoop as it will stretch the fabric and leave a mark that may be difficult to remove.

- Plan your route around a chart, counting over short distances wherever possible to avoid mistakes.

- Work your cross stitch in two directions in a sewing movement – half cross stitch in one direction and then cover those original stitches with the second row. This forms single vertical lines on the back that are very neat and give somewhere to finish raw ends. For neat work the top stitches should all face the same direction.

- If adding a backstitch outline, always add it after the cross stitch has been completed to prevent the solid line being broken.

QUICK STITCH COUNTS (see Calculating Design Size, page 14)										
	STITCH COUNT									
FABRIC	20	30	40	50	60	70	80	90	100	110
11-count Aida & 22-count evenweave	1¾in (4.6cm)	2¾in (7cm)	3⅝in (9.2cm)	4½in (11.5cm)	5½in (13.8cm)	6¼in (16cm)	7¼in (18.5cm)	8⅛in (20.7cm)	9in (23cm)	10in (25.4cm)
14-count Aida & 28-count evenweave	1½in (3.6cm)	2⅛in (5.4cm)	2¾in (7.2cm)	3½in (9cm)	4¼in (10.8cm)	5in (12.7cm)	5¾in (14.5cm)	6½in (16.3cm)	7⅛in (18cm)	7⅞in (20cm)
16-count Aida & 32-count evenweave	1¼in (3cm)	1¾in (4.8cm)	2½in (6.3cm)	3⅛in (8cm)	3¾in (9.5cm)	4¼in (11cm)	5in (12.7cm)	5½in (14.3cm)	6¼in (16cm)	6¾in (17.4cm)
18-count Aida & 36-count evenweave	1⅛in (2.8cm)	1½in (4.2cm)	2¼in (5.6cm)	2¾in (7cm)	3⅜in (8.5cm)	3¾in (9.8cm)	4½in (11.3cm)	5in (12.7cm)	5½in (14cm)	6⅛in (15.5cm)

THE STITCHES

ALGERIAN EYE

This star-shaped stitch is a pulled stitch which creates 'holes' in the fabric. It can be worked over two or four threads of evenweave and is more successful on evenweave than Aida.

Start to the left of a vertical thread and work from left to right around each stitch in an anticlockwise direction (or vice versa but keeping each stitch the same). Pass the needle down through the central hole and pull quite firmly so a small hole is formed in the centre. Take care that trailing threads do not cover the hole as you progress.

BACKSTITCH

Backstitch is used for outlining, to add detail or emphasis and for lettering. It is added after the cross stitch to prevent the backstitch line being broken. It is usually indicated on a chart by solid lines with the suggested shade on the chart or key.

Follow the numbered sequence, right, working the stitches over one block of Aida or two threads of evenweave.

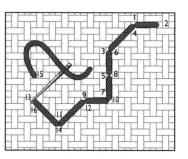

CROSS STITCH

This simple little stitch is the most commonly used stitch in this book. Cross stitches can be worked singly or in two journeys but for neat stitching, keep the top stitch facing the same direction. It does not matter which way it faces but it should be the same for the whole project.

CROSS STITCH ON AIDA

Cross stitch on Aida fabric is normally worked over one block.

To work one complete cross stitch
Follow the numbered sequence in the diagram: bring the needle up through the fabric at the bottom left corner, cross one block of the fabric and insert the needle at the top right corner. Push the needle

through and bring it up at the bottom right corner, ready to complete the stitch in the top left corner. To work the adjacent stitch, bring the needle up at the bottom right-hand corner of the first stitch.

To work cross stitches in two journeys
Work the first leg of the cross stitch as above but instead of completing the stitch, work the adjacent half stitch and continue on to the end of the row. Complete all the crosses by working the other diagonals on the return journey.

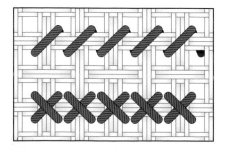

CROSS STITCH ON EVENWEAVE

Cross stitch on evenweave is usually worked over two threads of the fabric in each direction to even out any oddities in the thickness of the fibres. Bring the needle up to the left of a vertical thread, which will make it easier to spot counting mistakes. Work your cross stitch in two directions, as described before. This forms neat, single vertical lines on the back and gives somewhere to finish raw ends.

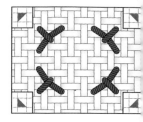

THREE-QUARTER CROSS STITCH

Three-quarter cross stitch is a fractional stitch which produces the illusion of curves when working cross stitch designs. The stitch can be formed on either Aida or evenweave but is more successful on evenweave. They are usually shown on charts as a triangle (half square).

Work the first half of a cross stitch as usual. Work the second 'quarter' stitch over the top and down into the central hole to anchor the first half of the stitch. If using Aida, you will need to push the needle through the centre of a block of the fabric. Where two three-quarter stitches lie back-to-back in the space of one full cross stitch, work both of the respective 'quarter' stitches into the central hole.

Some designs use half cross stitch and quarter cross stitch and these are, respectively, a single diagonal line and a quarter of a diagonal line.

FRENCH KNOT

French knots are shown on charts as circles, coloured on colour charts. Bring the needle through to the front of the fabric and wind the thread around the needle twice. Put the needle partly through to the back, one thread or part of a block away from the entry point, to stop the stitch being pulled to the wrong side. Gently pull the thread you have wound so that it sits snugly at the point where the needle enters the fabric. Pull the needle through to the back and you should have a perfect knot in position. For bigger knots, add more thread to the needle.

LONG STITCH

This is a long, straight stitch used to create animals' whiskers and so on. Bring the needle and thread up where the stitch is to start and down where the chart indicates it should finish. Occasionally long stitches are couched down – that is, held in place along its length with little stitches, as shown here.

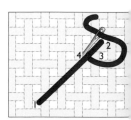

TENT STITCH

This stitch is usually used for working with wool (yarn) on canvas. It looks like half cross stitch from the front but has long, slanting stitches on the back, which

means it uses more yarn and thus is harder wearing. Follow the diagram, taking the needle under the stitches from right to left.